A Guide to the National Conveyancing Protocol

7 Day

A Guide to the National Conveyancing Protocol

FOURTH EDITION

TransAction 2001

The Law Society

The Law Society

© The Law Society 2001

ISBN 1 85328 731 8

1st edition 1990
2nd edition 1992
3rd edition 1994
4th edition 2001
Reprinted 2001

Published by the Law Society
113 Chancery Lane,
London WC2A 1PL

Typeset by Columns Design Ltd, Reading
Printed by Antony Rowe Ltd, Chippenham, Wilts

Contents

vi

Introduction

This book contains an easy-to-use guide to the Protocol which is now in its fourth edition. The guide details the revisions that have been made to improve the Protocol procedures in line with best practice.

In the past the Protocol concentrated on dealings between the two firms of solicitors involved and not with clients including lenders. The Protocol now covers dealings with the solicitor's client and has also been amended where necessary in view of the recent changes in the Practice Rules (Rule 6(3)(c) and Rule 15) and the introduction of the CML Lenders' Handbook.

The Law Society is committed to improving conveyancing standards and to improving communication between the profession and their clients as evidenced by Rule 15 of the Solicitors' Practice Rules 1990 and the Solicitors' Costs Information and Client Care Code 1999.

The text of the forms used in connection with the Protocol are included in this book together with explanatory guidance on how they should be used. The Seller's Property Information Form has been revised and now comprises one form with the first section to be completed by the seller and the second (shorter section) to be completed by the seller's solicitor. This is in response to representations from the profession that Part II of the Seller's Property Information Form was in places repetitive and was unnecessary.

The Seller's Leasehold Information Form has been updated and amended in a similar manner. Again there is only one form but with two sections.

The Fixtures, Fittings and Contents Form now includes two questions previously included on the Seller's Property Information Form.

An amended Completion Information and Requisitions on Title Form is included (revised 1998) which sets out in more detail the undertakings to be given on completion. This form should be signed only by a principal in the firm or someone who has authority to give undertakings on behalf of the firm.

As with previous editions, this book has been split into sections for ease of reference. Keep it to hand on your desk and make sure all conveyancing members of staff have their own copy.

March 2001

1. Use of the Protocol

Adopting the Protocol

The National Conveyancing Protocol TransAction 2001 (the Protocol) is designed for use in domestic conveyancing transactions of freehold and leasehold property. The Protocol is a form of 'preferred practice' and its requirements should not be construed as undertakings. They are not intended to widen a solicitor's duty except as mentioned in the next paragraph. The Protocol must always be considered in the context of a solicitor's overriding duty to his or her own client's interests. Where compliance with the Protocol would conflict with that duty, the client's wishes must always be paramount.

A solicitor acting in domestic conveyancing transactions should inform the solicitor acting for the other party at the outset of a transaction, whether or not the solicitor is proposing to act in accordance with the Protocol in full or in part. If the solicitor is using the Protocol the solicitor should give notice to the solicitor acting for the other party if during the course of the transaction it becomes necessary to depart from Protocol procedures.

Client confidentiality

A solicitor is, as a matter of professional conduct, under a duty to keep confidential client's business. The confidentiality continues until the client permits disclosure or waives confidentiality (Principle 16 in *The Guide to the Professional Conduct of Solicitors 1999*, published by the Law Society). With reference to paragraphs 4.7 and 5.8 of the Protocol, the disclosure of information about a client's position is strictly subject to obtaining that client's authority to disclose. In the absence of such authority, a solicitor is deemed not to be departing from the terms of the Protocol and is not required to give notice as set out in the preceding paragraph. The solicitor is however recommended to advise the client of the merits of using the Protocol to avoid unnecessary delays and of the advantage of all those involved in the transaction, or in other sales and purchases in the chain, being fully informed of progress on all matters at all times. Consequently clients should be encouraged to withhold the authority to disclose in exceptional circumstances only. However a solicitor's duty to the client remains and the client's wishes must always be paramount unless to comply with those wishes would be in breach of the Solicitors' Practice Rules 1990 (e.g. issuing a second contract without giving notice to the first buyer).

What is the Protocol?

The aim of the Protocol is to ensure that when the draft contract is submitted the buyer has as much information as possible about the property in the hope of narrowing the time gap between acceptance of an offer and actual exchange of contracts. It is hoped that this will assist in avoiding both gazumping and gazundering.

The Protocol contains the steps to be followed in a conveyancing transaction when it is adopted by a solicitor. The aim of these steps is to ensure that the seller's solicitor provides the buyer's solicitor with the relevant legal information about the property (other than the local authority search) as soon as possible after a suitable offer has been received. It must be stressed that the steps set out in the Protocol are not exhaustive and should not be regarded as a conveyancing 'checklist'.

The Protocol is to be used in conjunction with the forms described on pp. 4–8 and illustrated on pp. 34–63.

What is TransAction?

Some practitioners have become confused over the use of the term 'Protocol' and the term 'TransAction'. The Protocol describes the conveyancing procedures to be adopted by solicitors and licensed conveyancers who wish to use the Protocol in conveyancing transactions. TransAction 2001 is the marketing or brand name for these procedures and is the name which is used by solicitors who wish to publicise themselves to the public and their clients as users of the Protocol.

The use of the word TransAction and the logo is exclusive to solicitors. Licensed conveyancers cannot use the name or the logo, but they can use the forms provided they acknowledge on the forms the Law Society's copyright.

The Protocol timetable

The Protocol is designed to help streamline and speed up the conveyancing process. If it is possible and appropriate for a solicitor to anticipate future steps in the procedure, this is to be encouraged. Where the period between exchange of contracts and completion is very short, the delivery of a draft transfer is likely to be helpful prior to exchange of contracts and in some instances the seller's solicitor may be prepared to draft a document as part of the contract package. The effect of section 3 of the Law of Property (Miscellaneous Provisions) Act 1989, is to encourage the seller's solicitor to stipulate in the contract that the title is to be accepted. In such cases, the buyer's solicitor will wish to raise requisitions on title in advance of the Protocol timetable. The buyer's solicitor needs to consider carefully in any given case whether it is appropriate for the contract to contain a condition accepting title and to be mindful of the requirements of lenders and their solicitors when doing so. It is important to remember that the lender providing the mortgage funds to the buyer will not be bound by such a condition in the contract.

Solicitor–client relationship

The Law Society is committed to raising conveyancing standards and improving communication between the profession and their clients. Solicitors are reminded that in addition to adopting the Protocol they are also required to ensure that they adhere to Solicitors' Practice Rule 15 and Solicitors' Costs Information and Client Care Code 1999 (which now incorporates the written professional standards) and have regard to any guidance issued by the Law Society from time to time relating to conveyancing. A skeleton of a suggested contract report has now been included which can be adapted to suit the particular purchase. A more detailed contract report is set out in the Law Society's *Conveyancing Handbook 2001* (8th edition) at C1 'Preparing to Exchange'. It is recommended that all conveyancers should have a copy of, or at least access to, the latest edition of the Law Society's *Conveyancing Handbook*. It is updated and republished regularly.

2. Forms and Enquiries

Reproduction of forms

Copyright of the Seller's Property Information Form, the Seller's Leasehold Information Form, the Fixtures, Fittings and Contents Form and the Completion Information and Requisitions on Title Form rests in the Law Society. A general licence has been granted to the profession to reproduce these forms by word processor or in printed form. The Agreement for Sale (but not the Standard Conditions themselves) may also be reproduced by solicitors on word processors or in printed form. When any of these forms are reproduced in this manner they must display the following words in a prominent position:

'This form is part of the Law Society's TransAction scheme.'

This guarantees to one solicitor that the other solicitor has not departed from the approved wording of the form. These documents are available for purchase from the Law Society.

In previous editions of the Protocol, the client questionnaires (the Seller's Property Information Form Part I and the Seller's Leasehold Information Form Part I) were not permitted to be reproduced and to do so was in breach of the Law Society's copyright. The object of this was to ensure that all TransAction forms which were sent to the client were of uniform quality and appearance. It is hoped that the profession will ensure when reproducing any of the forms mentioned above that they are reproduced on quality paper.

The forms must be set out in the manner in which they have been produced by the Law Society to ensure uniformity.

The contract incorporating the Standard Conditions of Sale (third edition) front and back sheet may be reproduced by word processor but the Standard Conditions of Sale themselves may not be reproduced. To do so would be in breach of the joint copyright of the Law Society and the Solicitors' Law Stationery Society Ltd (Oyez). A Client Guide to the

Standard Conditions of Sale (third edition) is now available for purchase, setting out the Standard Conditions of Sale on a back-to-back sheet.

Practitioners are encouraged to utilise the forms listed above which provide a standardised method of carrying out conveyancing work and are designed to assist solicitors to offer a streamlined service to the public. Practitioners should take care to use the most up-to-date version of each form. If the most recent form is not used, a buyer's solicitor should consider whether to extract any of the revised or new questions from the latest form and raise them as additional enquiries.

Seller's Property Information Form

The Seller's Property Information Form is a condensed form of 'preliminary enquiries' from which has been removed all questions which are more appropriately dealt with by someone else. If any one part of the conveyancing process over the past years has caused criticism within the profession it has been the use of ever-lengthening forms of enquiries before contract, some being a repeat of those included in the standard form and others being irrelevant to the particular transaction or relating to the state or condition of the property. This is a matter for the valuer/surveyor.

The Seller's Property Information Form has been updated to take into account representations made since the third edition of the Protocol was produced. Part II of the form has been omitted, leaving two sections, the first of which needs to be completed by the client selling the property and the second section by the solicitor.

It is essential for the solicitor to check the information given by the client in Part I with the information in the deeds or in the seller's solicitor's possession.

The Protocol indicates the circumstances in which it is reasonable for the buyer's solicitor to raise additional enquiries relating to the property.

Seller's Leasehold Information Form

The Seller's Leasehold Information Form has been updated and also has two sections, the first section for completion by the seller and the second section for completion by the seller's solicitor. It is essential for the solicitor to check the information given by the client with the information in the deeds or in the seller's solicitor's possession. The seller's solicitor should check the papers in his possession for copy documents that the seller has been unable to provide and should indicate if a copy of a missing document will be supplied in due course.

Additional enquiries before contract

Practitioners are urged to raise only those additional enquiries that are needed in each particular transaction or locality and to resist the temptation to ask additional general enquiries especially those relating to the state and condition of the property. Experience has shown that many solicitors in the past refused to answer such questions on the grounds that the buyer took the property in its then state and condition and should rely on a professional survey. Preliminary enquiries should not therefore be raised relating to the state and condition of the property.

It is recommended that a buyer should always be advised that the property is purchased in its present state and condition and that the obtaining of an independent surveyor's report should be considered.

Buyers should be warned about relying on a valuation made for or on behalf of any lender.

There is no restriction on users of the Protocol raising relevant additional enquiries particularly those arising out of the documents provided with the draft contract.

A buyer's solicitor who sends a sheet of standard additional enquiries is not adhering to the terms and spirit of the Protocol.

Fixtures, Fittings and Contents Form

This form sets out in detail which items are, or are not, to be included in the sale of the property. It is suggested that this form is either sent to the client for completion at the same time as the Seller's Property Information Form or immediately when a buyer has been found.

The form should then be attached to the draft contract and forwarded by the seller's solicitor to the buyer's solicitor.

Agreement and Standard Conditions of Sale

The Agreement incorporates the Standard Conditions of Sale (third edition). Copyright in the Agreement and the Standard Conditions rests jointly in the Law Society and the Solicitors' Law Stationery Society Limited (Oyez). The Standard Conditions (third edition) which came into effect in 1995 are in plain English. Forms of the new standard Agreement are available with the full text of the Standard Conditions printed as part of it.

The Law Society Council Statement issued in 1990 with the first edition of the Protocol indicated that the use of the full form of contract was desirable and that this practice should be adopted rather than incorporating the Standard Conditions by reference. However, solicitors who produce their contracts on word processors or in printed form are permitted to reproduce the standard agreement, incorporating the Standard Conditions of Sale by reference only. Reproduction of the Standard Conditions themselves is not permitted.

Whilst the Standard Conditions of Sale were drafted for both domestic and commercial transactions they have been used mainly for domestic transactions. Standard Commercial Property Conditions have now been produced but they do not form part of the Protocol and should not be used in domestic transactions.

The National Conditions of Sale (twentieth edition) and the Law Society Conditions of Sale 1984 are no longer published and are not safe to rely upon since they have not been, and will not be, updated. The Standard Conditions of Sale replaced both those sets of conditions. The Standard Conditions of Sale (third edition) forms the twenty-third edition of the National Conditions of Sale and the 1995 edition of the Law Society's Conditions of Sale. Practitioners are encouraged to use the latest edition of the Standard Conditions of Sale as part of the process of standardising documentation.

The purpose of standardised documentation is to simplify the checking of variables. Accordingly solicitors using the Protocol should use the Agreement and Standard Conditions of Sale but ultimately it is a matter for the parties to decide upon the terms of their contract and relevant special conditions can be added as appropriate. It is strongly recommended that these variations and additions should be kept to a minimum.

Completion Information and Requisitions on Title Form

This form is designed to ensure solicitors are aware of the danger of giving thoughtless undertakings to discharge mortgages, hence the many warnings on the form. It is recommended that the form should only be signed by partners or solicitors or members of staff having authority to sign undertakings on behalf of the firm.

Solicitors may reproduce this form on their word processors providing the reproduction is exact and complete. The following words need to appear at the end of the form:

'This form is part of the Law Society's TransAction scheme.'

3. Searches

Local authority searches

There is no requirement under the Protocol for the seller's solicitor to make and supply a local authority search with the draft contract. However if the seller is anxious to eliminate delay before exchange of contracts and so reduce the risk of gazumping the seller's solicitor may suggest to the client that a local authority search with enquiries is carried out together with any other relevant searches so that these (or copies) can be supplied to the buyer's solicitor as part of the contract package.

Mining and other relevant searches

Again it will be up to the seller's solicitor to decide, if it is appropriate, whether to suggest to the seller that mining and any other relevant searches should be made on behalf of the seller so that these can be supplied to the buyer's solicitor as part of the contract package. The same applies to a commons registration search and to drainage and environmental enquiries.

Index map search

If the title to the seller's property is unregistered the seller's solicitor should make an index map search (see also Section 4).

The cost of searches

If the seller's solicitor has made any relevant searches and supplied either the original or copies to the buyer's solicitor then it is not against the ethos of the Protocol to ask that the buyer should, either on exchange of contracts or completion, reimburse the search fees incurred on behalf of the seller. If the seller wishes to be reimbursed for the search fees a special condition should be included in the contract. The local authority search should not be more than three months' old at exchange of contracts and six months' old at completion.

Office copies/epitome of title

Under the terms of the Protocol, the seller's solicitor is to provide the buyer with up-to-date office copy entries or, whilst they are awaited, a photocopy of the land or charge certificate if available. If the title is unregistered then the seller's solicitor should supply an examined epitome of title with an index map search.

Solicitors are reminded of the dangers of relying on copy entries which have been taken from the land or charge certificate itself (which may not be up-to-date) or on copy entries from which information has been deleted.

The seller's solicitor may be reluctant to send the original office copy entries to the buyer's solicitor. The seller's solicitor would not be in breach of the Protocol if an *examined copy* of the office copy entries was supplied with an *examined copy* of any document referred to in the land or charge certificate. Alternatively the original office copies can be sent to the buyer's solicitor to be held to the order of the seller's solicitor.

It is suggested that if original office copies or the original of any other document (including searches) is supplied to the buyer's solicitor, the seller's solicitor should make it clear when submitting the draft contract and other papers, that they are to be held to the order of the seller's solicitor, pending exchange of contracts. In the event of the transaction not proceeding, the buyer's solicitor must immediately return the draft contract and other papers to the seller's solicitor. If documents are sent to a solicitor subject to the condition that they are to be held to the sender's order, the recipient is subject to an implied undertaking that the documents will be returned on demand.

Original documents which are held subject to an undertaking to a mortgagee should not be sent to the buyer's solicitor as this would be in breach of that undertaking.

The original office copy entries should be handed over on exchange of contracts.

Some solicitors attempt to pass the duty and/or cost of obtaining office copy entries to the buyer. The buyer's solicitors are encouraged to resist

any such attempt. It is the seller's duty to deduce title at his own expense –
see the Law Society's *Conveyancing Handbook 2001* (8th edition).

4. Use of the Protocol by house builders' solicitors

There are a few steps in the Protocol which solicitors acting for developers may feel are inappropriate. However, when submitting a draft contract, many developers' solicitors at present include replies to the former standard preliminary enquiries, an information form, office copy entries or an epitome of title, together with a draft transfer.

With suitable amendments, the Seller's Property Information Form can be used and it is recommended that the developer's solicitor should do so. The developer's solicitor is also encouraged to use the contract incorporating the Standard Conditions of Sale adding such special conditions as may be necessary to cover, for example, the National House-Building Council's Buildmark Scheme and the building completion date. The Law Society's *Conveyancing Handbook 2001* recommends that the developer's solicitor should provide a package which includes these documents.

If the title or any part is unregistered it is also recommended that the developer's solicitor should make an index map search to cover the whole of the area over which rights are to be granted and to supply a copy of it with the contract package.

Where a development is made up of many plots the developer's solicitor should consider making a local land charges search of the whole scheme and supplying an examined copy to the solicitors acting for the buyer of each plot.

The buyer's solicitor will however need to consider making a local authority search relating to the particular plot to comply, for example, with any lender's requirements.

Use of the Protocol will help developers to obtain an early exchange of contracts and it is hoped that their solicitors will encourage them to adopt it. The modifications they make to the procedures are to be notified to the buyer's solicitor at the outset.

5. Deposits and insurance

Deposits

The Protocol and the Standard Conditions of Sale recognise the existing practice in many areas for the deposit received on the sale of the property to be used to pay the deposit on the purchase of another property.

The presence of Condition 2.2.3 may mean that a special condition will be necessary if Formula C is used on exchange of contracts and the person at the end of the chain will not agree to the deposit being held as stakeholder. In this event, it would be necessary for all parties in the chain to be notified and a special condition would be required only in the last contract in the chain. It is suggested that this should be:

> 'Standard Conditions 2.2.2 and 2.2.3 shall not apply and the deposit shall be paid to the seller's solicitor as agent for the seller.'

Where the deposit or any part of it is proposed to be held by the seller's solicitor as 'agent of the seller, the buyer-client should be advised of the risks involved in agreeing to this.

The Protocol envisages the deposit being passed by the buyer's solicitor to the seller's solicitor. Solicitors are reminded of the Law Society's Guidance on Property Fraud (see the 'Green card' warning on property fraud – practice information). In many cases of fraud, the deposit is allegedly paid direct between the parties. A solicitor should not confirm to another solicitor that deposit payments have been made or received unless the monies have been paid into that solicitor's client account or that solicitor has actual evidence that the payment has been made or received by a third party. The solicitor may need to inform the buyer's lender if there is no evidence of the payment of a deposit. Solicitors are reminded of Principle 16.01 in *The Guide to the Professional Conduct of Solicitors 1999*. Any solicitor with a query about a suspected mortgage fraud should contact the Law Society's Practice Advice Service on 0870 606 2522.

Property insurance

Under step 5.20 of the Protocol, the buyer's solicitor is responsible for ensuring that buildings insurance arrangements are in place. Where under the Standard Conditions of Sale the buyer relies upon the seller's insurance to cover damage to the property, it is recommended that the buyer's solicitor should inform the seller's solicitor of the amount of insurance cover which the buyer's surveyor or lender advises as a suitable level of insurance cover.

It is appreciated that many lenders do cover a property under a block policy from the date of exchange of contracts or the date of issue of the mortgage offer and, in such situations, double insurance of the property has not been avoided.

For those solicitors who, having considered the advantages and disadvantages of Standard Condition 5.1 and then decide not to adopt it, the following courses would appear to be open to them:

(1)   Condition 5.1 can be excluded altogether and the parties concerned can rely on the common law and section 47 of the Law of Property Act 1925. In this event a special condition would need to be added to the contract in the following form:

'Standard Condition 5.1 shall not apply.'

(2)   Alternatively Condition 5.1 could be accepted in the main but with the seller being put under an obligation to insure. In this event the following special condition should be added to the contract:

'Standard Condition 5.1.3 shall not apply and the seller shall continue the existing insurance of the property until actual completion.'

It would be essential for the seller to check that the property is insured for its full replacement value.

The seller could, if necessary, ask the buyer's solicitor if the surveyor or lender had advised on the amount of the insurance cover so that the seller is certain that the insurance cover on the property is adequate.

(3)   Another alternative would be to revert to the situation under the former Law Society's Conditions of Sale and to amend the Standard Conditions as follows:

'Standard Conditions 5.1.1 and 5.1.2 shall not apply and the following condition shall be substituted:

5.1.1 The property is at the buyer's risk as from the date of this contract.

5.1.2 If
   (a) the property suffers physical damage after the contract is made but before actual completion; and
   (b) the proceeds of any insurance policy taken out by or on behalf of the buyer are reduced because of insurance taken out by or on behalf of the seller;
the sum payable on completion is to be reduced by the amount of that reduction.

5.1.3 Condition 5.1.2 does not apply to the extent that the proceeds of the seller's policy are used to pay for reinstating the property as a result of any statutory or contractual obligation.'

Whilst the Protocol is a form of 'preferred practice' and recommends the use of the Standard Conditions of Sale, the solicitor must use his knowledge and judgement and act in the best interests of the client. It is hoped, however, that Standard Condition 5.1 will be used without amendment. If however it is felt that the condition does require some amendment alternative (3) above would appear to be appropriate for use in most contracts.

6. Other matters

The Law Society's Interest Rate

The Standard Conditions of Sale refer to the Law Society's Interest Rate. This replaces the rate of interest in the old Conditions of Sale which was calculated under the Land Compensation Act 1961. Many practitioners found this rate unhelpful and invariably inserted their own rate of interest into the contract by way of a special condition. The Law Society's rate is set at 4 per cent above the base rate from time to time of the Law Society's bankers.

This is published regularly in the Law Society's Gazette and is displayed in The Law Society's Hall, 113 Chancery Lane, London WC2A 1PL. Instead of prescribing their own rate by way of a special condition, conveyancers are encouraged to insert 'Law Society's interest rate' in the space provided on the front page of the Agreement.

TransAction logo

Wherever the logo is reproduced both the design and colour (pantone blue no. 294) must be retained. However, it has been agreed that where the logo is reproduced in a publication where spot colour is not available, the logo may be produced in black. The only other exception to the requirement is that solicitors may reproduce the logo in black and white on their notepaper. Where a firm wishes to indicate their inclusion in the TransAction scheme and not use the logo, they may do so by using the agreed wording:

'A member of the Law Society's TransAction scheme.'

Strict adherence to these guidelines will ensure that the logo and scheme have maximum consumer impact.

The Law Society's *Conveyancing Handbook*

In 1992 the Law Society's Land Law and Conveyancing Committee commissioned a handbook on conveyancing. The *Conveyancing Handbook* has been and will be updated on a regular basis. The Committee's aim was for the author to produce a book which would assist all conveyancing practitioners with their practical problems. It is not a book which seeks to challenge legal text books, such as *Emmet on Title*, but rather one which deals with everyday difficulties encountered by conveyancing practitioners and on which the Law Society gives daily telephone and written advice. The *Conveyancing Handbook* contains a full text on the various aspects of all conveyancing transactions in chronological sequence. Topics within each stage are clearly labelled for easy reference.

The *Conveyancing Handbook* provides checklists and suggests guidelines to help busy practitioners follow an efficient routine. Examples of checklists provided include:

- Matters raised at first interview;
- Preparing for exchange;
- Creation of a new mortgage.

It also contains a model form of a report on the contract.

At the back of the *Conveyancing Handbook* are comprehensive appendices containing among other things Law Society guidance on property matters, and the current edition of the National Conveyancing Protocol.

Assistance with further queries

The Law Society's Practice Advice Service is available to answer enquiries on the use of the Protocol.

Orders for books published by the Law Society can be placed through their distributors, Marston Book Services, tel. 01235 465656. For more information on other titles available from Law Society Publishing, please visit the Law Society's website at www.lawsociety.org.uk or call 020 7316 5599.

Appendices

The National Conveyancing Protocol (Fourth Edition)

ACTING FOR THE SELLER

1. The first step

The seller should inform the solicitor as soon as it is intended to place the property on the market so that delay may be reduced after a prospective purchaser is found.

2. Preparing the package: assembling the information

On receipt of instructions, the solicitor should then immediately take the following steps, at the seller's expense:

2.1 Whenever possible instructions should be obtained from the client in person.

2.2 Check the client's identity if the client is not known to you.

2.3 Give the client information as to costs, information relating to the name and status of the person who will be carrying out the work and, if that person is not a partner, the name of the partner who has overall responsibility for the matter. Give any other information necessary to comply with Rule 15 of the Solicitors' Practice Rules 1990 and Solicitors' Costs Information and Client Care Code 1999. If given orally this information should be confirmed in writing.

2.4 Give the seller details of whom to contact in the event of a complaint about the firm's services (Rule 15).

2.5 Consider with the client whether to make local authority and other searches so that these can be supplied to the buyer's solicitor as soon as an offer is made. If thought appropriate request a payment on account in relation to disbursements.

2.6 Ascertain the whereabouts of the deeds and, if not in the solicitor's custody, obtain them.

2.7 Ask the seller to complete the Seller's Property Information Form.

2.8 Obtain such original guarantees with the accompanying specification, planning decisions, building regulation approvals and certificates of completion as are in the seller's possession and copies of any other planning consents that are with the title deeds or details of any highway and sewerage agreements and bonds or any other relevant certificates relating to the property (e.g. structural engineer's certificate or an indemnity policy).

2.9 Give the seller the Fixtures, Fittings and Contents Form, with a copy to retain, to complete and return prior to the submission of the draft contract.

2.10 If the title is unregistered make an index map search.

2.11 If so instructed requisition a local authority search and enquiries and any other searches (e.g. mining or commons registration searches).

2.12 Obtain details of all mortgages and other financial charges of which the seller's solicitor has notice including, where applicable, improvement grants and discounts repayable to a local authority. Redemption figures should be obtained at this stage in respect of all mortgages on the property so that cases of negative equity or penalty redemption interest can be identified at an early stage.

2.13 Ascertain the identity of all people aged 17 or over living in the dwelling and ask about any financial contribution they or anyone else may have made towards its purchase or subsequent improvement. All persons identified in this way should be asked to confirm their consent to the sale proceeding.

2.14 In leasehold cases, ask the seller to complete the Seller's Leasehold Information Form and to produce, if possible:

(1) A receipt or evidence from the landlord of the last payment of rent.

(2) The maintenance charge accounts for the last three years, where appropriate, and evidence of payment.

(3) Details of the buildings insurance policy.

If any of these are lacking, and are necessary for the transaction, the solicitor should obtain them from the landlord. At the same time investigate whether a licence to assign is required and, if so, enquire of the landlord what references or deeds of covenant are necessary and, in the case of some retirement schemes, if a charge is payable to the management company on change of ownership.

3. Preparing the package: the draft documents

As soon as the title deeds are available, and the seller has completed the Seller's Property Information Form and, if appropriate, the Seller's Leasehold Information Form, the solicitor shall:

3.1   If the title is unregistered:

(1) Make a land charges search against the seller and any other appropriate names.

(2) Make an index map search in the Land Registry (if not already obtained – see 2.10) in order to verify that the seller's title is unregistered and ensure that there are no interests registered at the Land Registry adverse to the seller's title.

(3) Prepare an epitome of title. Mark copies or abstracts of all deeds which will not be passed to the buyer's solicitor as examined against the original.

(4) Prepare and mark as examined against the originals copies of all deeds, or their abstracts, prior to the root of title containing covenants, easements, etc., affecting the property.

(5) Check that all plans on copied documents are correctly coloured.

3.2   If the title is registered, obtain office copy entries of the register and copy documents incorporated or referred to in the certificate.

3.3 Prepare the draft contract and complete the second section of the Seller's Property Information Form and, if appropriate, the Seller's Leasehold Information Form.

3.4 Check contract package is complete and ready to be sent out to the buyer's solicitor.

3.5 Deal promptly with any queries raised by the estate agent.

4. Buyer's offer accepted

When made aware that a buyer has been found the solicitor shall:

4.1 Check with the seller agreement on the price and, if appropriate, that there has been no change in the information already supplied (Seller's Property Information Form, Seller's Leasehold Information Form and Fixtures, Fittings and Contents Form). Also check the seller's position on any related purchase.

4.2 Inform the buyer's solicitor that the Protocol will be used.

4.3 Ascertain the buyer's position on any related sale and in the light of that reply, ask the seller for a proposed completion date.

4.4 Send to the buyer's solicitor as soon as possible the contract package to include:

(1) Draft contract.

(2) Office copy entries of the registered title (including office copies of all documents mentioned), or the epitome of title (including details of any prior matters referred to but not disclosed by the documents themselves) and the index map search.

(3) The Seller's Property Information Form with copies of all relevant planning decisions, guarantees, etc.

(4) The completed Fixtures, Fittings and Contents Form. Where this is provided it will form part of the contract and should be attached to it.

(5) In leasehold cases:

(i) the Seller's Leasehold Information Form, with all information about maintenance charges and insurance and, if appropriate, the procedure (including references

24

required) for obtaining the landlord's consent to the sale;

(ii) a copy of the lease.

(6) If available, the local authority search and enquiries and any other searches made by the seller's solicitor.

If any of these documents are not available the remaining items should be forwarded to the buyer's solicitor as soon as they are available.

4.5   Inform the estate agent when the draft contract has been submitted to the buyer's solicitor.

4.6   Ask the buyer's solicitor if a 10 per cent deposit will be paid and, if not, what arrangements are proposed.

4.7   If and to the extent that the seller consents to the disclosure, supply information about the position on the seller's own purchase and of any other transactions in the chain above, and thereafter, of any change in circumstances.

4.8   Notify the seller of all information received in response to the above.

4.9   Inform the estate agent of any unexpected delays or difficulties likely to delay exchange of contracts.

ACTING FOR THE BUYER

5. The first step

On notification of the buyer's purchase the solicitor should then immediately take the following steps, at the buyer's expense:

5.1   Wherever possible instructions should be obtained from the client in person.

5.2   Check the client's identity if the client is not known to you.

5.3   Give the client information as to costs, information relating to the name and status of the person who will be carrying out the work and, if that person is not a partner, the name of the partner who has overall responsibility for the matter. Give any other information necessary to comply with Rule 15 of the Solicitors' Practice Rules 1990 and Solicitors' Costs Information and Client Care Code 1999. If given orally this information should be confirmed in writing.

5.4 Give the client details of whom to contact in the event of a complaint about the firm's services (Rule 15).

5.5 Request a payment on account in relation to disbursements.

5.6 Confirm to the seller's solicitor that the Protocol will be used.

5.7 Ascertain the buyer's position on any related sale, mortgage arrangements and whether a 10 per cent deposit will be provided.

5.8 If and to the extent that the buyer consents to the disclosure, inform the seller's solicitor about the position on the buyer's own sale, if any, and of any connected transactions, the general nature of the mortgage application, the amount of deposit available and if the seller's target date for completion can be met, and thereafter, of any change in circumstances.

On receipt of the draft contract and other documents:

5.9 Notify the buyer that these documents have been received, check the price and send the client a copy of the Fixtures, Fittings and Contents Form and, if appropriate, a copy of the filed plan for checking.

5.10 Make a local authority search with the usual part one enquiries and any additional enquiries relevant to the property.

5.11 Make a commons registration search, if appropriate.

5.12 Make mining enquiries and drainage enquiries if appropriate and consider any other relevant searches, e.g. environmental searches.

5.13 Check the buyer's position on any related sale and check that the buyer has a satisfactory mortgage offer and all conditions of the mortgage are or can be satisfied.

5.14 Check the buyer understands the nature and effect of the mortgage offer and duty to disclose any relevant matters to the lender.

5.15 Advise the buyer of the need for a survey on the property.

5.16 Confirm approval of the draft contract and return it approved as soon as possible, having inserted the buyer's full names and address, subject to any outstanding matters.

5.17 At the same time ask only those specific additional enquiries which are required to clarify some point arising out of the documents submitted or which are relevant to the particular nature or location of the property or which the buyer has expressly requested. Any enquiry, including those about the state and condition of the building, which is capable of being ascertained by the buyer's own enquiries or survey or personal inspection should not be raised. Additional duplicated standard forms should not be submitted; if they are, the seller's solicitor is under no obligation to deal with them nor need answer any enquiry seeking opinions rather than facts.

5.18 If a local authority search has been supplied by the seller's solicitors with the draft contract, consider the need to make a local authority search with the usual part one enquiries and any additional enquiries relevant to the property. (The local authority search should not be more than three months' old at exchange of contracts nor six months' old at completion.)

5.19 Ensure that buildings insurance arrangements are in place.

5.20 Check the position over any life policies referred to in the lender's offer of mortgage.

5.21 Check with the buyer if the property is being purchased in sole name or jointly with another person. If a joint purchase check whether as joint tenants or tenants in common and advise on the difference in writing.

BOTH PARTIES' SOLICITORS

6. Prior to exchange of contracts

If acting for the buyer

When all satisfactory replies received to enquiries and searches:

6.1 Prepare and send to the buyer a contract report and invite the buyer to make an appointment to call to raise any queries on the contract report and to sign the contract ideally in the presence of a solicitor.

6.2 When the buyer signs the contract check:

(1) Completion date.

(2) That the buyer understands and can comply with all the conditions on the mortgage offer if appropriate.

(3) That all the necessary funds will be available to complete the purchase.

If acting for the seller

6.3 Advise the seller on the effect of the contract and ask the seller to sign it, ideally in the presence of the solicitor.

6.4 Check the position on any related purchase so that there can be a simultaneous exchange of contracts on both the sale and purchase.

6.5 Check completion date.

7. Relationship with the buyer's lender

On receipt of instructions from the buyer's lender:

7.1 Check the mortgage offer complies with Practice Rule 6(3)(c) and (e) and is certified to that effect.

7.2 Check any special conditions in the mortgage offer to see if there are additional instructions or conditions not normally required by Practice Rule 6(3)(c).

7.3 Go through any special conditions in the mortgage offer with the buyer.

7.4   Notify the lender if Practice Rule 6(3)(b) or 1.13 or 1.14 of the CML Lenders' Handbook ('Lenders' Handbook') are applicable.

7.5   Consider whether there are any conflicts of interest which prevent you accepting instructions to act for the lender.

7.6   If you do not know the borrower and anyone else required to sign the mortgage, charge or other document, check evidence of identity (Practice Rule 6(3)(c)(i)).

7.7   Consider whether there are any circumstances covered by the Law Society's:

(1) Green Card on property fraud.

(2) Blue Card on money laundering.

(3) Pink Card on undertakings.

7.8   If you do not know the seller's solicitor/licensed conveyancer check that they appear in a legal directory or are on the record of their professional body (see Practice Rule 6(3)(c)(i) and the Lenders' Handbook).

7.9   Carry out any other checks required by the lender provided they comply with Practice Rule 6(3)(c).

7.10 At all times comply with the requirements of Practice Rule 6(3) and the Lenders' Handbook and ensure if a conflict of interest arises you cease to act for the lender.

8. Exchange of contracts

On exchange, the buyer's solicitor shall send or deliver to the seller's solicitor:

8.1   The signed contract with all names, dates and financial information completed.

8.2   The deposit provided in the manner prescribed in the contract. Under the Law Society's Formula C the deposit may have to be sent to another solicitor nominated by the seller's solicitor.

8.3   If contracts are exchanged by telephone the procedures laid down by the Law Society's Formulae A, B or C must be used and both solicitors must ensure (unless otherwise agreed) that the undertakings to send documents and to pay the deposit on that day are strictly observed.

8.4 The seller's solicitor shall, once the buyer's signed contract and deposit are held unconditionally, having ensured that the details of each contract are fully completed and identical, send the seller's signed contract on the day of exchange to the buyer's solicitor in compliance with the undertaking given on exchange.

8.5 Notify the client that contracts have been exchanged.

8.6 Notify the seller's estate agent or property seller of exchange of contracts and the completion date.

9. Between exchange and the day of completion

As soon as possible after exchange and in any case within the time limits contained in the Standard Conditions of Sale:

9.1 The buyer's solicitor shall send to the seller's solicitor, in duplicate:

(1) Completion Information and Requisitions on Title Form.

(2) Draft conveyance/transfer or assignment incorporating appropriate provisions for joint purchase.

(3) Other documents, e.g. draft receipt for purchase price of fixtures, fittings and contents.

9.2 As soon as possible after receipt of these documents the seller's solicitor shall send to the buyer's solicitor:

(1) Replies to Completion Information and Requisitions on Title Form.

(2) Draft conveyance/transfer or assignment approved.

(3) If appropriate, completion statement supported by photocopy receipts or evidence of payment of apportionments claimed.

(4) Copy of licence to assign from the landlord if appropriate.

9.3 The buyer's solicitor shall then:

(1) Engross the approved draft conveyance/transfer or assignment.

(2) Explain the effect of that document to the buyer and obtain the buyer's signature to it (if necessary).

(3) Send it to the seller's solicitor in time to enable the seller to sign it before completion without suffering inconvenience.

(4) If appropriate prepare any separate declaration of trust, advise the buyer on its effect and obtain the buyer's signature to it.

(5) Advise the buyer on the contents and effect of the mortgage deed and obtain the buyer's signature to that deed. If possible, and in all cases where the lender so requires, a solicitor should witness the buyer's signature to the mortgage deed.

(6) Send the certificate of title (complying with Rule 6(3)(d)) to the lender.

(7) Take any steps necessary to ensure that the amount payable on completion will be available in time for completion including sending to the buyer a completion statement to include legal costs, Land Registry fees and other disbursements and, if appropriate, stamp duty.

(8) Make the Land Registry and land charges searches and, if appropriate, a company search.

9.4 The seller's solicitor shall:

(1) Request redemption figures for all financial charges on the property revealed by the deeds/office copy entries/land charges search against the seller.

(2) On receipt of the engrossment of the conveyance/transfer or assignment, after checking the engrossment to ensure accuracy, obtain the seller's signature to it after ascertaining that the seller understands the nature and contents of the document. If the document is not to be signed in the solicitor's presence the letter sending the document for signature should contain an explanation of the nature and effect of the document and clear instructions relating to the execution of it.

(3) On receipt of the estate agent's or property seller's commission account obtain the seller's instructions to

pay the account on the seller's behalf out of the sale proceeds.

10. Relationship with the seller's estate agent or property seller

Where the seller has instructed estate agents or property seller, the seller's solicitor shall take the following steps:

10.1 Inform them when the draft contracts are submitted (see 4.5).

10.2 Deal promptly with any queries raised by them.

10.3 Inform them of any unexpected delays or difficulties likely to delay exchange of contracts (see 4.9).

10.4 Inform them when exchange has taken place and the date of completion (see 8.6).

10.5 On receipt of their commission account send a copy to the seller and obtain instructions as to arrangements for payment (see 9.4(3)).

10.6 Inform them of completion and, if appropriate, authorise release of any keys held by them (see 11.3(1)).

10.7 If so instructed pay the commission (see 9.4(3) and 11.6(2)).

11. Completion: the day of payment and removals

11.1 If completion is to be by post, the Law Society's Code for Completion shall be used, unless otherwise agreed.

11.2 As soon as practicable and not later than the morning of completion, the buyer's solicitor shall advise the seller's solicitor of the manner and transmission of the purchase money and of steps taken to despatch it.

11.3 On being satisfied as to the receipt of the balance of the purchase money, the seller's solicitor shall :

(1) Notify the estate agent or property seller that completion has taken place and authorise release of the keys.

(2) Notify the buyer's solicitor that completion has taken place and the keys have been released.

(3) Date and complete the transfer.

(4) Despatch the deeds including the transfer to the buyer's solicitor with any appropriate undertakings.

11.4 The seller's solicitor shall check that the seller is aware of the need to notify the local and water authorities of the change in ownership.

11.5 After completion, where appropriate, the buyer's solicitor shall give notice of assignment to the lessor.

11.6 Immediately after completion, the seller's solicitor shall:

(1) Send to the lender the amount required to release the property sold.

(2) Pay the estate agent's or property seller's commission if so authorised.

(3) Account to the seller for the balance of the sale proceeds.

11.7 Immediately after completion, the buyer's solicitor shall:

(1) Date and complete the mortgage document.

(2) Confirm completion of the purchase and the mortgage to the buyer.

(3) Pay stamp duty on the purchase deed, if appropriate.

(4) Deal with the registration of the transfer document and mortgage with the Land Registry within the priority period of the search.

(5) If appropriate, send a notice of assignment of a life policy to the insurance company.

(6) On receipt of the land or charge certificate from the Land Registry check its contents carefully and supply a copy of the certificate to the buyer.

(7) Send the charge certificate to the lender or deal with the land certificate in accordance with the buyer's instructions.

APPENDIX B
The forms

- Seller's Property Information Form (Prop. 1: revised 2001)

- Seller's Leasehold Information Form (Prop. 4: revised 2001)

- Fixtures, Fittings and Contents Form (Prop. 6: revised 2001)

- Completion Information and Requisitions on Title Form (Prop. 7: revised 1998)

- Agreement (Incorporating the Standard Conditions of Sale (Third Edition)) (1995)

SELLER'S PROPERTY INFORMATION FORM (2nd edition)

Address of the Property: _____

_____

_____

IMPORTANT NOTE TO SELLERS – PLEASE READ THIS FIRST

* Please complete this form carefully. If you are unsure how to answer the questions, ask your solicitor before doing so.

* This form in due course will be sent to the buyer's solicitor and will be seen by the buyer who is entitled to rely on the information.

* For many of the questions you need only tick the correct answer. Where necessary, please give more detailed answers on a separate sheet of paper. Then send all the replies to your solicitor. This form will be passed to the buyer's solicitor.

* The answers should be those of the person whose name is on the deeds. If there is more than one of you, you should prepare the answers together.

* It is very important that your answers are correct because the buyer is entitled to rely on them in deciding whether to go ahead. Incorrect or incomplete information given to the buyer direct through your solicitor or selling agent or even mentioned to the buyer in conversation between you, may mean that the buyer can claim compensation from you or even refuse to complete the purchase.

* If you do not know the answer to any question you must say so.

* The buyer takes the property in its present physical condition and should, if necessary, seek independent advice, e.g. instruct a surveyor. You should not give the buyer your views on the condition of the property.

* If anything changes after you fill in this questionnaire but before the sale is completed, tell your solicitor immediately. THIS IS AS IMPORTANT AS GIVING THE RIGHT ANSWERS IN THE FIRST PLACE.

* Please pass to your solicitor immediately any notices you have received which affect the property, including any notices which arrive at any time before completion of your sale.

* If you have a tenant, tell your solicitor immediately if there is any change in the arrangement but do nothing without asking your solicitor first.

* You should let your solicitor have any letters, agreements or other documents which help answer the questions. If you know of any which you are not supplying with these answers, please tell your solicitor about them.

* Please complete and return the separate Fixtures, Fittings and Contents Form. It is an important document which will form part of the contract between you and the buyer. Unless you mark clearly on it the items which you wish to remove, they will be included in the sale and you will not be able to take them with you when you move.

* You may wish to delay the completion of the Fixtures, Fittings and Contents Form until you have a prospective buyer and have agreed the price.

Prop 1/1

Part I – to be completed by the seller

1 | Boundaries

"Boundaries" means any fence, wall, hedge or ditch which marks the edge of your property.

1.1 Looking towards the house from the road, who either owns or accepts responsibility for the boundary:

Please mark the appropriate box

(a) on the left?

WE DO	NEXT DOOR	SHARED	NOT KNOWN

(b) on the right?

WE DO	NEXT DOOR	SHARED	NOT KNOWN

(c) across the back?

WE DO	NEXT DOOR	SHARED	NOT KNOWN

1.2 If you have answered "not known", which boundaries have you actually repaired or maintained?

(Please give details)

_____

_____

1.3 Do you know of any boundary being moved in the last 20 years?

(Please give details)

_____

_____

2 | Disputes and complaints

2.1 Do you know of any disputes or anything which might lead to a dispute about this or any neighbouring property?

NO	YES: (PLEASE GIVE DETAILS)

_____

_____

Prop 1/2

Please mark the appropriate box

2.2 Have you received any complaints about anything you have, or have not, done as owner?

NO	YES: (PLEASE GIVE DETAILS)

2.3 Have you made any such complaints to any neighbour about what the neighbour has or has not done?

NO	YES: (PLEASE GIVE DETAILS)

3 | Notices

3.1 Have you either sent or received any letters or notices which affect your property or the neighbouring property in any way (for example, from or to neighbours, the council or a government department)?

NO	YES:	COPY ENCLOSED	TO FOLLOW	LOST

3.2 Have you had any negotiations or discussions with any neighbour or any local or other authority which affect the property in any way?

NO	YES: (PLEASE GIVE DETAILS)

4 | Guarantees

4.1 Are there any guarantees or insurance policies of the following types:

(a) NHBC Foundation 15 or Newbuild?

NO	YES:	COPIES ENCLOSED	WITH DEEDS	LOST

(b) Damp course?

NO	YES:	COPIES ENCLOSED	WITH DEEDS	LOST

(c) Double glazing?

NO	YES:	COPIES ENCLOSED	WITH DEEDS	LOST

(d) Electrical work?

NO	YES:	COPIES ENCLOSED	WITH DEEDS	LOST

(e) Roofing?

NO	YES:	COPIES ENCLOSED	WITH DEEDS	LOST

Prop 1/3

37

Please mark the appropriate box

(f) Rot or infestation?

NO	YES:	COPIES ENCLOSED	WITH DEEDS	LOST

(g) Central heating?

NO	YES:	COPIES ENCLOSED	WITH DEEDS	LOST

(h) Anything similar, (e.g. cavity wall insulation, underpinning, indemnity policy)?

NO	YES:	COPIES ENCLOSED	WITH DEEDS	LOST

(i) Do you have written details of the work done to obtain any of these guarantees?

NO	YES:	COPIES ENCLOSED	WITH DEEDS	LOST

4.2 Have you made or considered making claims under any of these?

NO	YES: (PLEASE GIVE DETAILS)

4.3 Do you have a maintenance or service agreement for the central heating system?

NO	YES:	COPIES ENCLOSED	WITH DEEDS	LOST

5 Services

(This section applies to gas, electrical and water supplies, sewerage disposal and telephone cables.)

5.1 Please tick which services are connected to the property.

GAS	ELEC.	MAIN WATER	MAIN DRAINS	TEL.	CABLE TV	SEPTIC TANK/ CESSPIT

5.2 Please supply a copy of the latest water charge account and the sewerage account (if any).

ENCLOSED	TO FOLLOW

5.3 Is the water supply on a meter?

NO	YES

5.4 Do any drains, pipes or wires for these cross any neighbour's property?

NOT KNOWN	YES: (PLEASE GIVE DETAILS)

Prop 1/4

Please mark the appropriate box

5.5 Do any drains, pipes or wires leading to
any neighbour's property cross your property?

NOT KNOWN	YES: (PLEASE GIVE DETAILS)

_____

_____

5.6 Are you aware of any agreement or arrangement
about any of these services?

NOT KNOWN	YES: (PLEASE GIVE DETAILS)

_____

_____

6   Sharing with the neighbours

6.1 Are you aware of any responsibility
to contribute to the cost of anything used
jointly, such as the repair of a shared drive,
boundary or drain?

YES: (PLEASE GIVE DETAILS)	NO

_____

_____

6.2 Do you contribute to the cost of repair
of anything used by the neighbourhood,
such as the maintenance of a private road?

YES	NO

6.3 If so, who is responsible for organising
the work and collecting the contributions?

_____

_____

6.4 Please give details of all such sums paid
or owing, and explain if they are paid on a
regular basis or only as and when work is required.

_____

_____

6.5 Do you need to go on to any neighbouring
property if you have to repair or decorate your
building or maintain any of the boundaries or
any of the drains, pipes or wires?

YES	NO

Prop 1/5

39

6.6 If "Yes", have you always been able to do so without objection by the neighbours?

Please mark the appropriate box

YES	NO:	Please give details of any objection under the answer to question 2 (disputes)

6.7 Do any of your neighbours need to come onto your land to repair or decorate their building or maintain their boundaries or any drains, pipes or wires?

YES	NO

6.8 If so, have you ever objected?

NO	YES:	Please give details of any objection under the answer to question 2 (disputes)

7   Arrangements and rights

7.1 Is access obtained to any part of the property over private land, common land or a neighbour's land? If so, please specify.

NO	YES: (PLEASE GIVE DETAILS)

7.2 Has anyone taken steps to stop, complain about or demand payment for such access being exercised?

NO	YES

7.3 Are there any other formal or informal arrangements which you have over any of your neighbours' property?

(Examples are for access or shared use.)

NO	YES: (PLEASE GIVE DETAILS)

7.4 Are there any other formal or informal arrangements which someone else has over your property?

(Examples are for access or shared use.)

NO	YES: (PLEASE GIVE DETAILS)

Prop 1/6

40

Please mark the appropriate box

8 | Occupiers

8.1 Does anyone other than you live in the property?

If "NO" go to question 9.1.
If "YES" please give their full names and
(if under 18) their ages.

NO	YES

8.2(a)(i) Do any of them have any right to stay on
the property without your permission?

(These rights may have arisen without you realising,
e.g. if they have paid towards the cost of buying the
house, paid for improvements or helped you make
your mortgage payments.)

NO	YES: (PLEASE GIVE DETAILS)

8.2(a)(ii) Are any of them tenants or lodgers?

NO	YES: (Please give details and a copy of any Tenancy Agreement)

8.2(b) Have they all agreed to sign the contract
for sale agreeing to leave with you (or earlier)?

NO	YES: (PLEASE GIVE DETAILS)

9 | Changes to the property

9.1 Have any of the following taken place to the
whole or any part of the property (including the
garden) and if so, when?

(a) Building works (including loft conversions
and conservatories)

YES ...	NO

(b) Change of use

YES ...	NO

(c) Sub-division

YES ...	NO

(d) Conversion

YES ...	NO

Prop 1/7

41

Please mark the appropriate box

(e) Business activities

YES ...	NO

(f) Window replacement

YES ...	NO

If "YES" what consents were obtained under any restrictions in your title deeds?

(*Note*: The title deeds of some properties include clauses which are called "restrictive covenants". These may, for example, forbid the owner of the property from carrying out any building work or from using it for business purposes or from parking a caravan or boat on it unless someone else (often the builder of the house) gives consent.)

9.2 Has consent under those restrictions been obtained for anything else done at the property?

YES	NO

9.3 If any consent was needed but not obtained:

(a) Please explain why not.

(b) From whom should it have been obtained?

(*Note*: Improvements can affect council tax banding following a sale.)

---

10 | Planning and building control

10.1 Is the property used only as a private home?

YES	NO: (PLEASE GIVE DETAILS)

10.2(a) Has the property been designated as a Listed Building or the area designated as a Conservation Area? If so, when did this happen?

YES	NO	IN THE YEAR	NOT KNOWN

10.2(b) Was planning permission, building regulation approval or listed building consent obtained for each of the changes mentioned in 9?

NO	YES	COPY ENCLOSED	TO FOLLOW	LOST

(Please list separately and supply copies of the relevant permissions and, where appropriate, certificates of completion.)

Prop 1/8

42

Please mark the appropriate box

11 | Expenses

Have you ever had to pay for the use of the property?

NO	YES: (PLEASE GIVE DETAILS)

(Note: Ignore council tax, water rates, and gas, electricity, and telephone bills. Disclose anything else: examples are the clearance of cesspool or septic tank, drainage rate, rent charge.)

(If you are selling a leasehold property, details of the lease's expenses should be included on the Seller's Leasehold Information Form and not on this form.)

12 | Mechanics of the sale

12.1 Is this sale dependent on your buying another property?

YES	NO

12.2 If "YES", what stage have the negotiations reached?

12.3 Do you require a mortgage?

YES	NO

12.4 If "YES", has an offer been received and/or accepted or a mortgage certificate obtained?

YES	NO

13 | Deposit

Do you have the money to pay a 10% deposit on your purchase?

YES	NO

If "NO", are you expecting to use the deposit paid by your buyer to pay the deposit on your purchase?

YES	NO

Prop 1/9

43

Please mark the appropriate box

14	Moving date

Please indicate if you have any special requirement about a moving date.

YES	NO

(Note: This will not be fixed until contracts are exchanged i.e. have become binding. Until then you should only make provisional removal arrangements.)

Signature(s): ....

....

Date: ....

Prop 1/10

44

Part II – to be completed by the seller's solicitor

Please mark the appropriate box

A. Is the information provided by the seller in this form consistent with the information in your possession?

YES	NO

If "NO" please specify.

B. Do you have any information in your possession to supplement the information provided by the seller?

YES	NO

If "YES" please specify.

C. Is there an indemnity policy?

YES	NO

If "YES" please supply a copy.

Reminder to solicitor

1. The Fixtures, Fittings and Contents Form should be supplied in addition to the information above.

2. Copies of all planning permissions, building regulations consents, certificates of completion, engineer's certificates, guarantees, assignments, certificates and notices should be supplied with this form.

3. If the property is leasehold, also supply the Seller's Leasehold Information Form.

Seller's solicitor: ....

Date: ....

THE LAW SOCIETY

Prop 1/11

45

SELLER'S LEASEHOLD INFORMATION FORM (2nd edition)

Address of the Property:

_____

_____

If you live in leasehold property, please answer the following questions. Some people live in blocks of flats, others in large houses converted into flats and others in single leasehold houses. These questions cover all types of leasehold property, but some of them may not apply to your property. In that case, please answer them N/A.

The instructions set out at the front of the Seller's Property Information Form apply to this form as well. Please read them again before giving your answers to these questions.

If you are unsure how to answer any of the questions, ask your solicitor.

Part I – to be completed by the seller

1 | Management company

Please mark the appropriate box

1.1 If there is a management company which is run by the tenants please supply any of the following documents which are in your possession:

(a) Memorandum and articles of association of the company.

ENCLOSED	TO FOLLOW	LOST	WITH THE DEEDS	N/A

(b) Your share or membership certificate.

ENCLOSED	TO FOLLOW	LOST	WITH THE DEEDS	N/A

(c) The company's accounts for the last 3 years.

ENCLOSED	TO FOLLOW	LOST	WITH THE DEEDS	N/A

(d) Copy of any regulations made by either the landlord or the company additional to the rules contained in the lease.

ENCLOSED	TO FOLLOW	LOST	WITH THE DEEDS	N/A

(e) The names and addresses of the secretary and treasurer of the company.

_____

_____

(f) Has the management company been struck off the register at Companies House?

YES	NO	NOT KNOWN

Prop 4/1

Please mark the appropriate box

1.2 If the tenants do not run the Management
Company is there a Tenants' Association?

YES	NO

If "YES" please supply the contact name and
address.

2 The landlord

2.1 What is the name and address of your landlord?

2.2 If the landlord employs an agent to collect
the rent, what is the name and address of that agent?

2.3 Please supply a receipt from the landlord for
the last rent payment.

ENCLOSED	TO FOLLOW

3 Maintenance charges

3.1 Are you liable under your lease to pay a
share of the maintenance cost of the building?

YES	NO

If "NO" go to question 4.

3.2 Do you know of any expense (e.g.
redecoration of outside or communal areas not
usually incurred annually) likely to show in the
maintenance charge accounts within the next
3 years?

YES	NO

If "YES" please give details

3.3 Have maintenance charges been demanded
for each of the last 3 years?

YES	NO

3.4 If so, please supply the maintenance accounts
and receipts for these.

ENCLOSED	TO FOLLOW

3.5 Do you know of any problems in the last
3 years between flat owners and the landlord
or management company about maintenance
charges, or the method of management?

YES	NO

If "YES", please give details.

Prop 4/2

Please mark the appropriate box

3.6 Have you challenged the maintenance charge or any expense in the last 3 years?

YES	NO

If "YES", please give details.

_____

_____

3.7 Do you know if the landlord has had any problems in collecting the maintenance charges from other flat owners?

YES	NO

If "YES", please give details

_____

_____

4 Notices

A notice may be in a printed form or in the form of a letter and your buyer will wish to know if anything of this sort has been received.

4.1 Have you had a notice that the landlord wants to sell the building?

NO	YES:	ENCLOSED	TO FOLLOW

4.2 Have you had any other notice about the building, its use, its condition or its repair and maintenance?

NO	YES:	ENCLOSED	TO FOLLOW

5 Consents

Are you aware of any changes in the terms of the lease or of the landlord giving any consents under the lease? (This may be in a formal document, a letter or even oral.)

NO	YES:	ENCLOSED	TO FOLLOW

If not in writing, please supply details.

_____

_____

6 Complaints

6.1 Have you received any complaints from the landlord, any other landlord, management company or any other occupier about anything you have or have not done?

YES	NO

If "YES", please give details.

_____

_____

Prop 4/3

Please mark the appropriate box

6.2 Have you complained or had cause for complaint to or about any of them?

YES	NO

If "YES", please give details.

_____

_____

7 | Buildings insurance on the property

7.1 Are you responsible under the lease for arranging the buildings insurance on the property?

YES	NO

7.2 If "YES", please supply a copy of:

(a) the insurance policy and

COPY ENCLOSED	TO FOLLOW

(b) receipt for the last payment of the premium

COPY ENCLOSED	TO FOLLOW

7.3 If "NO", please supply a copy of the insurance policy arranged by the landlord or the management company and a copy of the schedule for the current year.

COPY ENCLOSED	TO FOLLOW

8 | Decoration

8.1 When was the outside of the building last decorated?

IN THE YEAR	NOT KNOWN

8.2 When were any internal, communal parts last decorated?

IN THE YEAR	NOT KNOWN

8.3 When was the inside of your property last decorated?

IN THE YEAR	NOT KNOWN

9 | Alterations

9.1 Are you aware of any alterations having been made to your property since the lease was originally granted?

YES	NO	NOT KNOWN

If "YES", please supply details.

_____

_____

9.2 If "YES", was landlord's consent obtained?

NO	NOT KNOWN	NOT REQUIRED	YES	COPIES ENCLOSED	TO FOLLOW

Prop 4/4

49

Please mark the appropriate box

10	Occupation

10.1 Are you now occupying the property as your sole or main home?

YES	NO

10.2 Have you occupied the property as your sole or main home (apart from usual holidays and business trips):

(a) continuously throughout the last 12 months?

YES	NO

(b) continuously throughout the last 3 years?

YES	NO

(c) for periods totalling at least 3 years during the last 10 years?

YES	NO

11	Enfranchisement

11.1 Have you served on the landlord or any other landlord a formal notice under the enfranchisement legislation stating your desire to buy the freehold or be granted an extended lease?

If so, please supply a copy.

NO	YES:	COPY ENCLOSED	COPY TO FOLLOW

11.2 If the property is a flat in a block, are you aware of the service of any notice under the enfranchisement legislation relating to the possible collective purchase of the freehold of the block or part of it?

NO	YES:	COPY ENCLOSED	COPY TO FOLLOW

11.3 Have you received any response to that notice?

NO	YES:	COPY ENCLOSED	COPY TO FOLLOW

Signature(s): ....

Date: ....

Part II – to be completed by the seller's solicitor

A. Is the information provided by the seller in this form consistent with the information in your possession?

If "NO", please specify.

YES	NO

Prop 4/5

Please mark the appropriate box

B. Do you have any information in your possession
to supplement the information provided by the seller?

YES	NO

If "YES", please specify.

_____

_____

_____

C. Please provide the name and address of the
recipient of notice of assignment and charge.

_____

_____

_____

D. Do the insurers make a practice of recording the
interest of the buyer's mortgagee and the buyer on
the policy?

YES	NO	NOT KNOWN

E. Please supply a copy of the Fire Certificate.

ENCLOSED	TO FOLLOW	NOT APPLICABLE

F. Are all of the units in the building or
development let on identical leases? If not, in
what respect do they differ?

YES	NO	NOT KNOWN

_____

_____

_____

G. Has the landlord experienced problems with
the collection of maintenance charges as they fall
due? If so, please supply details.

YES	NO	NOT KNOWN

_____

_____

H. Is the property part of a converted building?

NO	YES

If "YES", please supply a copy of the Planning
Permission or an Established Use Certificate, or
evidence of permitted use.

ENCLOSED	TO FOLLOW	NOT APPLICABLE

Reminder

**Copies of any relevant documents should be supplied with this form, e.g. memorandum and articles of association of the
company, share or membership certificate, management accounts for the last 3 years, copy of any regulations made either
by the landlord or the company additional to the rules contained in the lease, name and address of the secretary and treasurer of the company, and copies of any notices served upon the seller under sections 18–30 the Landlord and Tenant Act
1987, the Leasehold Reform Act 1967 or the Leasehold Reform Housing and Urban Development Act 1993.**

Seller's solicitor: ....

Date: ....

Prop 4/6

FIXTURES FITTINGS AND CONTENTS (3rd edition)

Address of the Property:

1. Place a tick in one of these three columns against every item.
2. The second column ("excluded from the sale") is for items on the list which you are proposing to take with you when you move. If you are prepared to sell any of these to the buyer, please write the price you wish to be paid beside the name of the item and the buyer can then decide whether or not to accept your offer to sell.

	INCLUDED IN THE SALE	EXCLUDED FROM THE SALE	NONE AT THE PROPERTY
TV Aerial/Satellite Dish			
Radio Aerial			
Immersion Heater			
Hot Water Cylinder Jacket			
Roof Insulation			
Wall Heaters			
Night Storage Heater			
Gas/Electric Fires			
Light Fittings:			
Ceiling Lights	☐	☐	☐
Wall Lights	☐	☐	☐
Lamp Shades	☐	☐	☐
N.B. If these are to be removed, it is assumed that they will be replaced by ceiling rose and socket, flex bulb holder and bulb.			
Switches			
Electric Points			
Dimmer Switches			
Fluorescent Lighting			
Outside Lights			

This form comprises 6 pages. Please ensure you complete all sections on all pages.   Please turn over to next page.   PROP6/1

	INCLUDED IN THE SALE	EXCLUDED FROM THE SALE	NONE AT THE PROPERTY
Telephone Receivers:			
British telecom	☐	☐	☐
Own	☐	☐	☐
Burglar Alarm System			
Complete Central Heating System			
Extractor Fans			
Doorbell/Chimes			
Door Knocker			
Door Furniture:			
Internal	☐	☐	☐
External	☐	☐	☐
Double Glazing			
Window Fitments			
Shutters/Grills			
Curtain Rails			
Curtain Poles			
Pelmets			
Venetian Blinds			
Roller Blinds			
Curtains (Including Net Curtains):			
Lounge	☐	☐	☐
Dining Room	☐	☐	☐
Kitchen	☐	☐	☐
Bathroom	☐	☐	☐

PROP6/2

APPENDIX B

	INCLUDED IN THE SALE	EXCLUDED FROM THE SALE	NONE AT THE PROPERTY
Bedroom 1	☐	☐	☐
Bedroom 2	☐	☐	☐
Bedroom 3	☐	☐	☐
Bedroom 4	☐	☐	☐
Other Rooms (state which)			
1	☐	☐	☐
2	☐	☐	☐
3	☐	☐	☐
Carpets and other Floor Covering:			
Lounge	☐	☐	☐
Dining Room	☐	☐	☐
Kitchen	☐	☐	☐
Hall, Stairs and Landing	☐	☐	☐
Bathroom	☐	☐	☐
Bedroom 1	☐	☐	☐
Bedroom 2	☐	☐	☐
Bedroom 3	☐	☐	☐
Bedroom 4	☐	☐	☐
Other Rooms (state which)			
1	☐	☐	☐
2	☐	☐	☐
3	☐	☐	☐

PROP6/3

54

FIXTURES, FITTINGS AND CONTENTS

	INCLUDED IN THE SALE	EXCLUDED FROM THE SALE	NONE AT THE PROPERTY
Storage Units in Kitchen			
Kitchen Fitments:			
Fitted Cupboards and Shelves	☐	☐	☐
Refrigerator/ fridge-Freezer	☐	☐	☐
Oven	☐	☐	☐
Extractor Hood	☐	☐	☐
Hob	☐	☐	☐
Cutlery Rack	☐	☐	☐
Spice Rack	☐	☐	☐
Other (state which)			
1	☐	☐	☐
2	☐	☐	☐
3	☐	☐	☐
Kitchen Furniture:			
Washing Machine	☐	☐	☐
Dishwasher	☐	☐	☐
Tumble-Drier	☐	☐	☐
Cooker	☐	☐	☐
Other (state which)			
1	☐	☐	☐
2	☐	☐	☐
3	☐	☐	☐

PROP6/4

55

	INCLUDED IN THE SALE	EXCLUDED FROM THE SALE	NONE AT THE PROPERTY
Bathroom Fitments:			
Cabinet	☐	☐	☐
Towel Rails	☐	☐	☐
Soap and Tooth-brush Holders	☐	☐	☐
Toilet Roll Holders	☐	☐	☐
Fitted Shelves/ Cupboards	☐	☐	☐
Other Sanitary Fittings	☐	☐	☐
Shower			
Shower Fittings			
Shower Curtain			
Bedroom Fittings:			
Shelves	☐	☐	☐
Fitted Wardrobes	☐	☐	☐
Fitted Cupboards			
Fitted Shelving/ Cupboards			
Fitted Units			
Wall Mirrors			
Picture Hooks			
Plant Holders			
Clothes Line			
Rotary Line			
Garden Shed			
Greenhouse			
Garden Ornaments			

PROP6/5

56

	INCLUDED IN THE SALE	EXCLUDED FROM THE SALE	NONE AT THE PROPERTY
Trees, Plants and Shrubs			
Garden Produce			
Stock of Oil/Solid Fuel/Propane Gas			
Water Butts			
Dustbins			
Other			

1. If you have sold through an estate agent, are all items listed in its particulars included in the sale?

If "No" you should instruct the estate agent to write to everyone concerned correcting this error.

Please tick the right answer

YES	NO

2. Do you own outright everything included in the sale?

(You must give details of anything which may not be yours to sell, for example, anything rented or on HP)

YES	NO: (PLEASE GIVE DETAILS)

....

....

NB: If you are removing any fixtures or fittings you must make good any damage caused.

You are also responsible for removing all your possessions, including rubbish, from the property, the garage and any outbuildings or sheds.

Signed Seller(s)

. . . .

. . . .

THE LAW SOCIETY

PROP6/6

COMPLETION INFORMATION AND REQUISITIONS ON TITLE

WARNING: Replies to Requisitions 4.2 and 6.2 are treated as a solicitor's undertaking.

Property: ....

Seller: ....

Buyer: ....

1. PROPERTY INFORMATION

Please confirm that the written information given by or on behalf of the seller prior to exchange of contracts is complete and accurate. (This includes SPIF Parts I and II, SLIF Parts I and II, Replies to Pre-Contract enquiries and correspondence between us.)

2. VACANT POSSESSION

2.1 If vacant possession is to be given on completion:-
   (a) What arrangements will be made to hand over the keys?
   (b) By what time will the Seller have vacated the property on the completion date?

2.2 If vacant possession is not being given, please confirm that an authority to the Tenant to pay the rent to the Buyer will be available at completion.

3. DEEDS

3.1 Do you hold all the title deeds? If not, where are they?

3.2 Please list the deeds and documents to be handed over on completion.

3.3 If the land/charge certificate is on deposit, what is the deposit number? If it is not deposit and will not be handed over on completion, please put it on deposit now and supply the deposit number on completion.

4. COMPLETION

4.1 Will completion take place at your office? If not, where will it take place?

4.2 If we wish to complete through the post, please confirm that:
   (a) you undertake to adopt the current Law Society's Code for Completion by Post, and

   (b) the mortgages and charges listed in reply to 6.1 are those specified for the purpose of paragraph 3 of the Code.

5. MONEY

5.1 Please state the exact amount payable on completion. If it is not just the balance purchase money, please provide copy receipts for any rent or service charge or other payments being apportioned.

Prop 7/1

Either

5.2   Please give:
        (a)   Name and address of your bank

        (b)   Sort Code
        (c)   Your Client Account Number to
                which monies are to be sent.

Or

5.3   State in whose favour a banker's draft should be drawn.

6.   UNDERTAKINGS

WARNING: **A reply to this requisition is treated as an undertaking. Great care must be taken when answering this requisition.**

6.1   Please list the mortgages or charges secured on the property which you undertake to redeem or discharge to the extent that they relate to the propety on or before completion (this includes repayment of any discount under the Housing Acts).

6.2   Do you undertake to redeem or discharge the mortgages and charges listed in reply to 6.1 on completion and to send to us Form DS1 or the receipted charges as soon as you receive them?

6.3   If you agree to adopt the current Law Society's Code for Completion by Post, please confirm that you are the duly authorised agent of the proprietor of every mortgage or charge on the property which you have undertaken, in reply to 6.2, to redeem or discharge.

....
                        Buyer's Solicitor   Seller's Solicitor

Date..   Date..

WARNING: These replies should be signed only by a person with authority to give undertakings on behalf of the firm

ADDITIONAL REQUISITIONS

Prop 7/2

AGREEMENT
(Incorporating the Standard Conditions of Sale (Third Edition))

Agreement date	:
Seller	:
Buyer	:
Property **(freehold/leasehold)**	:
Root of title/Title Number	:
Incumbrances on the Property	:
Title Guarantee **(full/limited)**	:
Completion date	:
Contract rate	:
Purchase price	:
Deposit	:
Amount payable for chattels	:
Balance	:

The Seller will sell and the Buyer will buy the Property for the Purchase price.

The Agreement continues on the back page.

WARNING	**Signed**
This is a formal document, designed to create legal rights and legal obligations. Take advice before using it.	Seller/Buyer

STANDARD CONDITIONS OF SALE (THIRD EDITION)

(NATIONAL CONDITIONS OF SALE 23rd EDITION, LAW SOCIETY'S CONDITIONS OF SALE 1995)

1. GENERAL

1.1 Definitions

1.1.1 In these conditions:
- (a) "accrued interest" means:
  - (i) if money has been placed on deposit or in a building society share account, the interest actually earned
  - (ii) otherwise, the interest which might reasonably have been earned by depositing the money at interest on seven days' notice of withdrawal with a clearing bank

  less, in either case, any proper charges for handling the money
- (b) "agreement" means the contractual document which incorporates these conditions, with or without amendment
- (c) "banker's draft" means a draft drawn by and on a clearing bank
- (d) "clearing bank" means a bank which is a member of CHAPS Limited
- (e) "completion date", unless defined in the agreement, has the meaning given in condition 6.1.1
- (f) "contract" means the bargain between the seller and the buyer of which these conditions, with or without amendment, form part
- (g) "contract rate", unless defined in the agreement, is the Law Society's interest rate from time to time in force
- (h) "lease" includes sub-lease, tenancy and agreement for a lease or sub-lease
- (i) "notice to complete" means a notice requiring completion of the contract in accordance with condition 6
- (j) "public requirement" means any notice, order or proposal given or made (whether before or after the date of the contract) by a body acting on statutory authority
- (k) "requisition" includes objection
- (l) "solicitor" includes barrister, duly certificated notary public, recognised licensed conveyancer and recognised body under sections 9 or 32 of the Administration of Justice Act 1985
- (m) "transfer" includes conveyance and assignment
- (n) "working day" means any day from Monday to Friday (inclusive) which is not Christmas Day, Good Friday or a statutory Bank Holiday.

1.1.2 When used in these conditions the terms "absolute title" and "office copies" have the special meanings given to them by the Land Registration Act 1925.

1.2 Joint parties

If there is more than one seller or more than one buyer, the obligations which they undertake can be enforced against them all jointly or against each individually.

1.3 Notices and documents

1.3.1 A notice required or authorised by the contract must be in writing.

1.3.2 Giving a notice or delivering a document to a party's solicitor has the same effect as giving or delivering it to that party.

1.3.3 Transmission by fax is a valid means of giving a notice or delivering a document where delivery of the original document is not essential.

1.3.4 Subject to conditions 1.3.5 to 1.3.7, a notice is given and a document delivered when it is received.

1.3.5 If a notice or document is received after 4.00pm on a working day, or on a day which is not a working day, it is to be treated as having been received on the next working day.

1.3.6 Unless the actual time of receipt is proved, a notice or document sent by the following means is to be treated as having been received before 4.00pm on the day shown below:

(a) by first-class post:	two working days after posting
(b) by second-class post:	three working days after posting
(c) through a document exchange:	on the first working day after the day on which it would normally be available for collection by the addressee.

1.3.7 Where a notice or document is sent through a document exchange, then for the purposes of condition 1.3.6 the actual time of receipt is:
- (a) the time when the addressee collects it from the document exchange or, if earlier
- (b) 8.00am on the first working day on which it is available for collection at that time.

1.4 VAT

1.4.1 An obligation to pay money includes an obligation to pay any value added tax chargeable in respect of that payment.

1.4.2 All sums made payable by the contract are exclusive of value added tax.

2. FORMATION

2.1 Date

2.1.1 If the parties intend to make a contract by exchanging duplicate copies by post or through a document exchange, the contract is made when the last copy is posted or deposited at the document exchange.

2.1.2 If the parties' solicitors agree to treat exchange as taking place before duplicate copies are actually exchanged, the contract is made as so agreed.

2.2 Deposit

2.2.1 The buyer is to pay or send a deposit of 10 per cent of the purchase price no later than the date of the contract. Except on a sale by auction, payment is to be made by banker's draft or by a cheque drawn on a solicitors' clearing bank account.

2.2.2 If before completion date the seller agrees to buy another property in England and Wales for his residence, he may use all or any part of the deposit as a deposit in that transaction to be held on terms to the same effect as this condition and condition 2.2.3.

2.2.3 Any deposit or part of a deposit not being used in accordance with condition 2.2.2 is to be held by the seller's solicitor as stakeholder on terms that on completion it is paid to the seller with accrued interest.

2.2.4 If a cheque tendered in payment of all or part of the deposit is dishonoured when first presented, the seller may, within seven working days of being notified that the cheque has been dishonoured, give notice to the buyer that the contract is discharged by the buyer's breach.

2.3 Auctions

2.3.1 On a sale by auction the following conditions apply to the property and, if it is sold in lots, to each lot.

2.3.2 The sale is subject to a reserve price.

2.3.3 The seller, or a person on his behalf, may bid up to the reserve price.

2.3.4 The auctioneer may refuse any bid.

2.3.5 If there is a dispute about a bid, the auctioneer may resolve the dispute or restart the auction at the last undisputed bid.

3. MATTERS AFFECTING THE PROPERTY

3.1 Freedom from incumbrances

3.1.1 The seller is selling the property free from incumbrances, other than those mentioned in condition 3.1.2.

3.1.2 The incumbrances subject to which the property is sold are:
- (a) those mentioned in the agreement
- (b) those discoverable by inspection of the property before the contract
- (c) those the seller does not and could not know about
- (d) entries made before the date of the contract in any public register except those maintained by HM Land Registry or its Land Charges Department or by Companies House
- (e) public requirements.

3.1.3 After the contract is made, the seller is to give the buyer written details without delay of any new public requirement and of anything in writing which he learns about concerning any incumbrances subject to which the property is sold.

3.1.4 The buyer is to bear the cost of complying with any outstanding public requirement and is to indemnify the seller against any liability resulting from a public requirement.

3.2 Physical state

3.2.1 The buyer accepts the property in the physical state it is in at the date of the contract unless the seller is building or converting it.

3.2.2 A leasehold property is sold subject to any subsisting breach of a condition or tenant's obligation relating to the physical state of the property which renders the lease liable to forfeiture.

3.2.3 A sub-lease is granted subject to any subsisting breach of a condition or tenant's obligation relating to the physical state of the property which renders the seller's own lease liable to forfeiture.

3.3 Leases affecting the property

3.3.1 The following provisions apply if the agreement states that any part of the property is sold subject to a lease.

3.3.2
- (a) The seller having provided the buyer with full details of each lease or copies of the documents embodying the lease terms, the buyer is treated as entering into the contract knowing and fully accepting those terms
- (b) The seller is to inform the buyer without delay if the lease ends or if the seller learns of any application by the tenant in connection with the lease; the seller is then to act as the buyer reasonably directs, and the buyer is to indemnify him against all consequent loss and expense
- (c) The seller is not to agree to any proposal to change the lease terms without the consent of the buyer and is to inform the buyer without delay of any change which may be proposed or agreed
- (d) The buyer is to indemnify the seller against all claims arising from the lease after actual completion; this includes claims which are unenforceable against a buyer for want of registration
- (e) The seller takes no responsibility for what rent is lawfully recoverable, nor for whether or how any legislation affects the lease
- (f) If the let land is not wholly within the property, the seller may apportion the rent.

3.4 Retained land

3.4.1 The following provisions apply where after the transfer the seller will be retaining land near the property.

3.4.2 The buyer will have no right of light or air over the retained land, but otherwise the seller and the buyer will each have the rights over the land of the other which they would have had if they were two separate buyers to whom the seller had made simultaneous transfers of the property and the retained land.

3.4.3 Either party may require that the transfer contain appropriate express terms.

4. TITLE AND TRANSFER

4.1 Timetable

4.1.1 The following are the steps for deducing and investigating the title to the property to be taken within the following time limits:

Step	Time Limit
1. The seller is to send the buyer evidence of title in accordance with condition 4.2	Immediately after making the contract
2. The buyer may raise written requisitions	Six working days after either the date of the contract or the date of delivery of the seller's evidence of title on which the requisitions are raised whichever is the later
3. The seller is to reply in writing to any requisitions raised	Four working days after receiving the requisitions
4. The buyer may make written observations on the seller's replies	Three working days after receiving the replies

The time limit on the buyer's right to raise requisitions applies even where the seller supplies incomplete evidence of his title, but the buyer may, within six working days from delivery of any further evidence, raise further requisitions resulting from that evidence. On the expiry of the relevant time limit the buyer loses his right to raise requisitions or make observations.

4.1.2 The parties are to take the following steps to prepare and agree the transfer of the property within the following time limits:

Step	Time Limit
A. The buyer is to send the seller a draft transfer	At least twelve working days before completion date
B. The seller is to approve or revise that draft and either return it or retain it for use as the actual transfer	Four working days after delivery of the draft transfer
C. If the draft is returned the buyer is to send an engrossment to the seller	At least five working days before completion date

4.1.3 Periods of time under conditions 4.1.1 and 4.1.2 may run concurrently.

4.1.4 If the period between the date of the contract and completion date is less than 15 working days, the time limits in conditions 4.1.1 and 4.1.2 are to be reduced by the same proportion as that period bears to the period of 15 working days. Fractions of a working day are to be rounded down except that the time limit to perform any step is not to be less than one working day.

4.2 Proof of title

4.2.1 The evidence of registered title is office copies of the items required to be furnished by section 110(1) of the Land Registration Act 1925 and the copies, abstracts and evidence referred to in section 110(2).

4.2.2 The evidence of unregistered title is an abstract of the title, or an epitome of title with photocopies of the relevant documents.

4.2.3 Where the title to the property is unregistered, the seller is to produce to the buyer (without cost to the buyer):
- (a) the original of every relevant document, or
- (b) an abstract, epitome or copy with an original marking by a solicitor of examination either against the original or against an examined abstract or against an examined copy.

4.3 Defining the property

4.3.1 The seller need not:
- (a) prove the exact boundaries of the property
- (b) prove who owns fences, ditches, hedges or walls
- (c) separately identify parts of the property with different titles

further than he may be able to do from information in his possession.

4.3.2 The buyer may, if it is reasonable, require the seller to make or obtain, pay for and hand over a statutory declaration about facts relevant to the matters mentioned in condition 4.3.1. The form of the declaration is to be agreed by the buyer, who must not unreasonably withhold his agreement.

4.4 Rents and rentcharges

The fact that a rent or rentcharge, whether payable or receivable by the owner of the property, has been or will on completion be, informally apportioned is not to be regarded as a defect in title.

4.5 Transfer

4.5.1 The buyer does not prejudice his right to raise requisitions, or to require replies to any raised, by taking any steps in relation to the preparation or agreement of the transfer.

4.5.2 If the agreement makes no provision as to title guarantee, then subject to condition 4.5.3 the seller is to transfer the property with full title guarantee.

4.5.3 The transfer is to have effect as if the disposition is expressly made subject to all matters to which the property is sold subject under the terms of the contract.

4.5.4 If after completion the seller will remain bound by any obligation affecting the property, but the law does not imply any covenant by the buyer to indemnify the seller against liability for future breaches of it:
(a) the buyer is to covenant in the transfer to indemnify the seller against liability for any future breach of the obligation and to perform it from then on, and
(b) if required by the seller, the buyer is to execute and deliver to the seller on completion a duplicate transfer prepared by the buyer.

4.5.5 The seller is to arrange at his expense that, in relation to every document of title which the buyer does not receive on completion, the buyer is to have the benefit of:
(a) a written acknowledgement of his right to its production, and
(b) a written undertaking for its safe custody (except while it is held by a mortgagee or by someone in a fiduciary capacity).

5. PENDING COMPLETION

5.1 Responsibility for property

5.1.1 The seller will transfer the property in the same physical state as it was at the date of the contract (except for fair wear and tear), which means that the seller retains the risk until completion.

5.1.2 If at any time before completion the physical state of the property makes it unusable for its purpose at the date of the contract:
(a) the buyer may rescind the contract
(b) the seller may rescind the contract where the property has become unusable for that purpose as a result of damage against which the seller could not reasonably have insured, or which it is not legally possible for the seller to make good.

5.1.3 The seller is under no obligation to the buyer to insure the property.

5.1.4 Section 47 of the Law of Property Act 1925 does not apply.

5.2 Occupation by buyer

5.2.1 If the buyer is not already lawfully in the property, and the seller agrees to let him into occupation, the buyer occupies on the following terms.

5.2.2 The buyer is a licensee and not a tenant. The terms of the licence are that the buyer:
(a) cannot transfer it
(b) may permit members of his household to occupy the property
(c) is to pay or indemnify the seller against all outgoings and other expenses in respect of the property
(d) is to pay the seller a fee calculated at the contract rate on the purchase price (less any deposit paid) for the period of the licence
(e) is entitled to any rents and profits from any part of the property which he does not occupy
(f) is to keep the property in as good a state of repair as it was in when he went into occupation (except for fair wear and tear) and is not to alter it
(g) is to insure the property in a sum which is not less than the purchase price against all risks in respect of which comparable premises are normally insured
(h) is to quit the property when the licence ends.

5.2.3 On the creation of the buyer's licence, condition 5.1 ceases to apply, which means that the buyer then assumes the risk until completion.

5.2.4 The buyer is not in occupation for the purposes of this condition if he merely exercises rights of access given solely to do work agreed by the seller.

5.2.5 The buyer's licence ends on the earliest of: completion date, rescission of the contract or when five working days' notice given by one party to the other takes effect.

5.2.6 If the buyer is in occupation of the property after his licence has come to an end and the contract is subsequently completed he is to pay the seller compensation for his continued occupation calculated at the same rate as the fee mentioned in condition 5.2.2(d).

5.2.7 The buyer's right to raise requisitions is unaffected.

6. COMPLETION

6.1 Date

6.1.1 Completion date is twenty working days after the date of the contract but time is not of the essence of the contract unless a notice to complete has been served.

6.1.2 If the money due on completion is received after 2.00pm, completion is to be treated, for the purposes only of conditions 6.3 and 7.3, as taking place on the next working day.

6.1.3 Condition 6.1.2 does not apply where the sale is with vacant possession of the property or any part and the seller has not vacated the property or that part by 2.00pm on the date of actual completion.

6.2 Place

Completion is to take place in England and Wales, either at the seller's solicitor's office or at some other place which the seller reasonably specifies.

6.3 Apportionments

6.3.1 Income and outgoings of the property are to be apportioned between the parties so far as the change of ownership on completion will affect entitlement to receive or liability to pay them.

6.3.2 If the whole property is sold with vacant possession or the seller exercises his option in condition 7.3.4, apportionment is to be made with effect from the date of actual completion; otherwise, it is to be made from completion date.

6.3.3 In apportioning any sum, it is to be assumed that the seller owns the property until the end of the day from which apportionment is made and that the sum accrues from day to day at the rate at which it is payable on that day.

6.3.4 For the purpose of apportioning income and outgoings, it is to be assumed that they accrue at an equal daily rate throughout the year.

6.3.5 When a sum to be apportioned is not known or easily ascertainable at completion, a provisional apportionment is to be made according to the best estimate available. As soon as the amount is known, a final apportionment is to be made and notified to the other party. Any resulting balance is to be paid no more than ten working days later, and if not then paid the balance is to bear interest at the contract rate from then until payment.

6.3.6 Compensation payable under condition 5.2.6 is not to be apportioned.

6.4 Amount payable

The amount payable by the buyer on completion is the purchase price (less any deposit already paid to the seller or his agent) adjusted to take account of:
(a) apportionments made under condition 6.3
(b) any compensation to be paid or allowed under condition 7.3.

6.5 Title deeds

6.5.1 The seller is not to retain the documents of title after the buyer has tendered the amount payable under condition 6.4.

6.5.2 Condition 6.5.1 does not apply to any documents of title relating to land being retained by the seller after completion.

6.6 Rent receipts

The buyer is to assume that whoever gave any receipt for a payment of rent or service charge which the seller produces was the person or the agent of the person then entitled to that rent or service charge.

6.7 Means of payment

The buyer is to pay the money due on completion in one or more of the following ways:
(a) legal tender
(b) a banker's draft
(c) a direct credit to a bank account nominated by the seller's solicitor
(d) an unconditional release of a deposit held by a stakeholder.

6.8. Notice to complete

6.8.1 At any time on or after completion date, a party who is ready able and willing to complete may give the other a notice to complete.

6.8.2 A party is ready able and willing:
(a) if he could be, but for the default of the other party, and
(b) in the case of the seller, even though a mortgage remains secured on the property, if the amount to be paid on completion enables the property to be transferred freed of all mortgages (except those to which the sale is expressly subject).

6.8.3 The parties are to complete the contract within ten working days of giving a notice to complete, excluding the day on which the notice is given. For this purpose, time is of the essence of the contract.

6.8.4 On receipt of a notice to complete:
(a) if the buyer paid no deposit, he is forthwith to pay a deposit of 10 per cent
(b) if the buyer paid a deposit of less than 10 per cent, he is forthwith to pay a further deposit equal to the balance of that 10 per cent.

7. REMEDIES

7.1 Errors and omissions

7.1.1 If any plan or statement in the contract, or in the negotiations leading to it, is or was misleading or inaccurate due to an error or omission, the remedies available are as follows.

7.1.2 When there is a material difference between the description or value of the property as represented and as it is, the injured party is entitled to damages.

7.1.3 An error or omission only entitles the injured party to rescind the contract:
(a) where it results from fraud or recklessness, or
(b) where he would be obliged, to his prejudice, to transfer or accept property differing substantially (in quantity, quality or tenure) from what the error or omission had led him to expect.

7.2 Rescission

If either party rescinds the contract:
(a) unless the rescission is a result of the buyer's breach of contract the deposit is to be repaid to the buyer with accrued interest
(b) the buyer is to return any documents he received from the seller and is to cancel any registration of the contract.

7.3 Late completion

7.3.1 If there is default by either or both of the parties in performing their obligations under the contract and completion is delayed, the party whose total period of default is the greater is to pay compensation to the other party.

7.3.2 Compensation is calculated at the contract rate on the purchase price, or (where the buyer is the paying party) the purchase price less any deposit paid, for the period by which the paying party's default exceeds that of the receiving party, or, if shorter, the period between completion date and actual completion.

7.3.3 Any claim for loss resulting from delayed completion is to be reduced by any compensation paid under this contract.

7.3.4 Where the buyer holds the property as tenant of the seller and completion is delayed, the seller may give notice to the buyer, before the date of actual completion, that he intends to take the net income from the property until completion. If he does so, he cannot claim compensation under condition 7.3.1 as well.

7.4 After completion

Completion does not cancel liability to perform any outstanding obligation under this contract.

7.5 Buyer's failure to comply with notice to complete

7.5.1 If the buyer fails to complete in accordance with a notice to complete, the following terms apply.

7.5.2 The seller may rescind the contract, and if he does so:
(a) he may
(i) forfeit and keep any deposit and accrued interest
(ii) resell the property
(iii) claim damages
(b) the buyer is to return any documents he received from the seller and is to cancel any registration of the contract.

7.5.3 The seller retains his other rights and remedies.

7.6 Seller's failure to comply with notice to complete

7.6.1 If the seller fails to complete in accordance with a notice to complete, the following terms apply.

7.6.2 The buyer may rescind the contract, and if he does so:
(a) the deposit is to be repaid to the buyer with accrued interest
(b) the buyer is to return any documents he received from the seller and is, at the seller's expense, to cancel any registration of the contract.

7.6.3 The buyer retains his other rights and remedies.

8. LEASEHOLD PROPERTY

8.1 Existing leases

8.1.1 The following provisions apply to a sale of leasehold land.

8.1.2 The seller having provided the buyer with copies of the documents embodying the lease terms, the buyer is treated as entering into the contract knowing and fully accepting those terms.

8.1.3 The seller is to comply with any lease obligations requiring the tenant to insure the property.

8.2 New leases

8.2.1 The following provisions apply to a grant of a new lease.

8.2.2 The conditions apply so that:
"seller" means the proposed landlord
"buyer" means the proposed tenant
"purchase price" means the premium to be paid on the grant of a lease.

8.2.3 The lease is to be in the form of the draft attached to the agreement.

8.2.4 If the term of the new lease will exceed 21 years, the seller is to deduce a title which will enable the buyer to register the lease at HM Land Registry with an absolute title.

8.2.5 The buyer is not entitled to transfer the benefit of the contract.

8.2.6 The seller is to engross the lease and a counterpart of it and is to send the counterpart to the buyer at least five working days before completion date.

8.2.7 The buyer is to execute the counterpart and deliver it to the seller on completion.

8.3 Landlord's consent

8.3.1 The following provisions apply if a consent to assign or sub-let is required to complete the contract.

8.3.2 (a) The seller is to apply for the consent at his expense, and to use all reasonable efforts to obtain it
(b) The buyer is to provide all information and references reasonably required.

8.3.3 The buyer is not entitled to transfer the benefit of the contract.

8.3.4 Unless he is in breach of his obligation under condition 8.3.2, either party may rescind the contract by notice to the other party if three working days before completion date:
(a) the consent has not been given or
(b) the consent has been given subject to a condition to which the buyer reasonably objects.

In that case, neither party is to be treated as in breach of contract and condition 7.2 applies.

9. CHATTELS

9.1 The following provisions apply to any chattels which are to be sold.

9.2 Whether or not a separate price is to be paid for the chattels, the contract takes effect as a contract for sale of goods.

9.3 Ownership of the chattels passes to the buyer on actual completion.

AGREEMENT (INCORPORATING THE STANDARD CONDITIONS OF SALE)

SPECIAL CONDITIONS

1. (a) This Agreement incorporates the Standard Conditions of Sale (Third Edition). Where there is a conflict between those Conditions and this Agreement, this Agreement prevails.

   (b) Terms used or defined in this Agreement have the same meaning when used in the Conditions.

2. The Property is sold subject to the Incumbrances on the Property and the Buyer will raise no requisitions on them.

3. Subject to the terms of this Agreement and to the Standard Conditions of Sale, the Seller is to transfer the property with the title guarantee specified on the front page.

4. The chattels on the Property and set out on any attached list are included in the sale.

5. The Property is sold with vacant possession on completion.

(or) 5. The Property is sold subject to the following leases or tenancies:

Seller's Solicitors   :

Buyer's Solicitors   :

©1995 **OYEZ** The Solicitors' Law Stationery Society Ltd,
Oyez House, 7 Spa Road, London SE16 3QQ

© 1995 **THE LAW SOCIETY**

1.97 F33188
5065046
*
3rd Edition

Standard Conditions of Sale

Contract report

This is only a skeleton of the information which it is suggested should be included in the contract report (see step 6.1 of the Protocol). A much fuller report on a proposed purchase is set out in the Law Society's Conveyancing Handbook *(section C1 'Preparing to exchange').*

REPORT ON PROPOSED PURCHASE

of the property known as

_____

Prepared for Mr and Mrs _____

1. The Property

The property is known as _____. A copy of the Land Registry plan is attached. The red line represents the extent of the property. The plan is to a small scale and so does not show the precise location of each boundary. You should check these at the property and any significant discrepancies should be referred to us.

2. Title

The property is freehold/leasehold. [*Note*: if the property is leasehold it will also be necessary to supply a copy of the lease and advise on its terms.]

The Title Number is _____. It is registered at the Land Registry with an absolute title.

3. Rights passing with the property

[*Set out details of rights enjoyed by the property and any liability to contribute towards expenses.*]

4. Rights over the property

[*Set out any rights affecting the property.*]

5. Covenants

[*Give details of any covenants both restrictive and positive affecting the property.*]

6. Information from the sellers

The solicitors acting for the sellers have supplied us with a package under the Law Society's TransAction Scheme. We attach copies of the following items supplied to us in that package:

(a) **Seller's Property Information Form**
[*Give details of any information on which comments are appropriate.*]

(b) **List of Fixtures, Fittings and Contents**
This indicates which items at the property are included in the sale and which are not. Please check that this is in accordance with your agreement with the sellers. [*Note*: with leasehold property a copy of the Seller's Leasehold Information Form should be supplied with such comments on it as are appropriate.]

7. Information from local authority

[*Comment on information revealed on local search and any other searches made.*]

65

8. The purchase contract

This is in a form incorporating the Standard Conditions of Sale which are widely used for this type of transaction. The main provisions of the contract are :

(a) Price.

(b) Deposit.

(c) Completion date.

(d) Interest rate.

(e) State and condition of the property.

(f) Insurance.

9. Mortgage

[*Give details of any mortgage instructions received and of the main terms.*]

10. Joint purchase

[*If there are two .or more buyers, enquire if they are purchasing as joint tenants or tenants in common and explain the difference.*]

11. Environmental or other matters

[*Give details.*]

Please ask us if you have any queries about this report (including any of the papers sent with it) or on any other aspect of your purchase.

May we ask you to telephone us to make an appointment to call to see us to raise such queries and to sign the contract.

(*Name of solicitors*)